WHAT'S FASTER THAN A SPEEDING CHEETAH?

Robert E. Wells

www.av2books.com

Fiction Readalong — AV² By Weigl™ — Added Value • Audio Visual

Your AV² Media Enhanced book gives you a fiction readalong online.
Log on to www.av2books.com and enter the unique book code from
this page to use your readalong.

Go to **www.av2books.com**, and enter this book's unique code.

BOOK CODE

H343008

AV² by Weigl brings you media enhanced books that support active learning.

First Published by

ALBERT WHITMAN & COMPANY
Publishing children's books since 1919

AV² Readalong Navigation

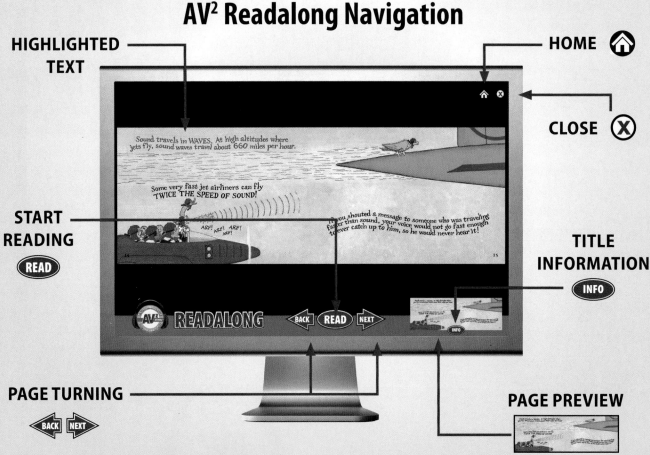

HIGHLIGHTED TEXT

HOME

CLOSE

START READING
READ

TITLE INFORMATION
INFO

PAGE TURNING
BACK NEXT

PAGE PREVIEW

You may very well be fast on your feet. But if you want to WIN races, never race a CHEETAH— or even an OSTRICH, for that matter.

3

If you ran very hard, you might reach a speed of 15 miles per hour.

That's not nearly fast enough to keep up with an ostrich. With a top speed of about 45 miles per hour, an ostrich is the world's fastest 2-legged runner.

But the cheetah will certainly be way out in front.

A cheetah can reach a speed of about 70 miles per hour – MORE THAN A MILE A MINUTE!

No animal on EARTH can run faster than that!

But a cheetah can't run nearly as fast as a PEREGRINE FALCON can SWOOP!

A peregrine falcon can dive through the sky at about 200 miles per hour!

That's 3 times as fast as a car zooming along a highway!

ARF!

ARF!

ARF!

A peregrine falcon is truly a SUPER SWOOPER.

It can dive faster than any creature can run.

FINISH

But not as fast as an AIRPLANE can fly!

Some propeller planes can fly more than **300** miles per hour.

With a propeller pulling you through the air, you can travel faster than the fastest falcon.

But with a JET ENGINE, you can fly faster than the fastest propeller plane – and even faster than the SPEED OF SOUND!

If you shouted a message to someone who was traveling faster than sound, your voice would not go fast enough to ever catch up to him, so he would never hear it!

Flying through the air in a jet
is a mighty fast way to travel.

But if you want to travel to the MOON, you're going to need something that's much, MUCH faster.

You're going to need a ROCKET SHIP!

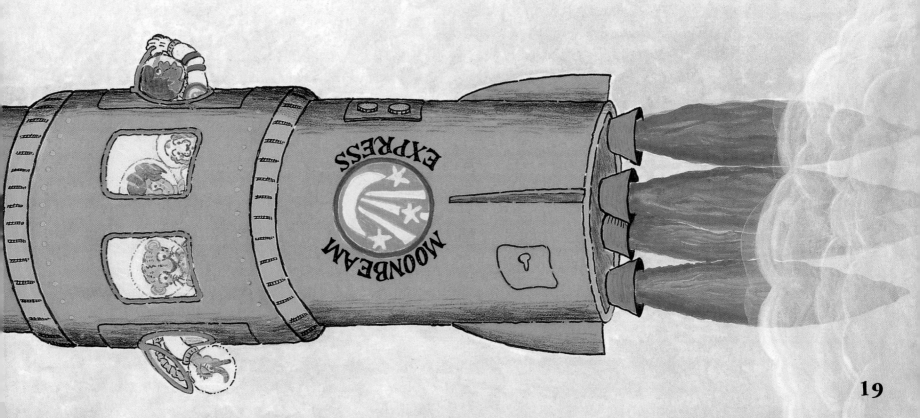

To escape Earth's gravity and travel into space, a rocket ship must travel faster than the fastest jet.

To travel all the way to the moon, a rocket ship must reach a speed of about 25,000 MILES PER HOUR—MORE THAN 30 TIMES AS FAST AS SOUND!

You can turn off your rockets and COAST after you're in space, because there's no air friction.

Now speeding through space at 25,000 miles per hour is mighty fast. But what's THAT zooming by, going so much faster you feel like you're standing still?

MOONBEAM EXPRESS

22

IT'S A METEOROID!

A meteoroid is a space rock. Some meteoroids streak through space at 150,000 miles per hour— SIX TIMES FASTER THAN YOUR ROCKET SHIP IS TRAVELING!

23

As you circle around the moon and head back to Earth, you might be thinking that the meteoroid you saw was the absolute fastest thing you could ever see.

But hold on a minute. There's something much faster than even the fastest meteoroid— and it's something you see all the time.

Instantly, a **LIGHT BEAM** will flash out at the amazing speed of **186,000** miles per **SECOND!**

That's **THOUSANDS** of times **FASTER THAN A METEOROID!**

At that speed, you could circle the Earth **MORE THAN 7 TIMES IN ONE SECOND!**

Most scientists believe that nothing can travel through space faster than light.

Who ever would have thought that the FASTEST TRAVELING THING IN THE WHOLE UNIVERSE could come out of something small enough to hold in your hand?

Some Additional Thoughts on Very Fast Things

Sometimes speeds are hard to measure. Observers often have trouble measuring the speeds of wild animals, so books may have numbers that differ. The figures given in this book seem to be the best estimates. It would be much simpler if cheetahs, ostriches, and falcons came with speedometers!

The speed of sound through air is easier to measure than the speeds of wild animals. But the speed of sound is not constant. It's about 760 miles per hour at sea level but slows to about 660 miles per hour at high altitudes where the air is thin and cold.

Meteoroids zoom through space at different speeds, too. The meteoroid in this book is one of the faster ones.

The amazing speed of light, traveling through space at 186,000 miles per second, is one of the few speeds you can count on to be constant.

All the speeds in this book are true to life, but some liberties were taken in the illustrations to better show speed comparisons. In the real world, supersonic jets fly much higher than little propeller planes. And large meteoroids don't often narrowly miss rocket ships!

Although light beams flashing through space are usually shown as bright rays, as is the one in this book, a real light beam becomes bright and visible only when hitting such things as dust or water particles. Fortunately, our space travelers happened to be zooming through a big cloud of space dust just as they switched on their flashlight!

At This Speed	How Long Would It Take to Travel
YOUNG RUNNER (15 MILES PER HOUR)	
OSTRICH (45 MPH)	
CHEETAH (70 MPH)	
PEREGRINE FALCON (200 MPH)	
PROPELLER PLANE (300 MPH)	
SUPERSONIC JET (1400 MPH)	
ROCKET SHIP (25,000 MPH)	
METEOROID (150,000 MPH)	
LIGHT (186,000 MILES PER SECOND)	

30

FROM THE EARTH TO THE MOON?
(ABOUT 239,000 MILES)

	IT WOULD TAKE ABOUT
	1¾ YEARS
	7⅓ MONTHS
	4⅔ MONTHS
	7 WEEKS
	4⅔ WEEKS
	1 WEEK
	9½ HOURS
	1½ HOURS
	1⅓ SECONDS

31

Published by AV² by Weigl
350 5ᵗʰ Avenue, 59ᵗʰ Floor New York, NY 10118

Copyright ©2013 AV² by Weigl

Printed in the United States of America in North Mankato, Minnesota
1 2 3 4 5 6 7 8 9 0 16 15 14 13 12

Published in 1997 by Albert Whitman & Company.

052012
WEP160512

Library of Congress Cataloging-in-Publication Data

Wells, Robert E.
What's faster than a speeding cheetah? / by Robert E. Wells.
    p. cm.
ISBN 978-1-61913-153-8 (hard cover : alk. paper)
1. Speed--Juvenile literature. I. Title.
QC137.52.W45 2013
531'.11--dc23
                        2012017287